Please return my book

OF RODENTS AND PERSONS

Bette Ann Coyle

B. Counting on Frank Rod Clement's delightful story about a boy who uses fact, figures, and his own wild imagination to make counting fun. Appendix includes an introduction to the metric system, thought-provoking measurement activities, and answers. Hardcover. 32 pages.

COUNTING on FRANK

Meet Frank's owner, the quick-witted narrator of ***Counting on Frank.*** Call him a measuring maniac or a fool for figuring, but this young man surely has a unique way of looking at the world. From peas to ballpoint pens, everything takes on a new — and hilarious — significance when he examines it. And, in the back of the book, you'll have an opportunity to look at **your** world in the same detail — from macaroni to how fast you grow. Enjoy the adventure!

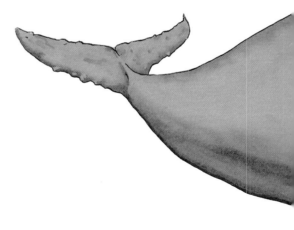

For a free color catalog describing Gareth Stevens' list of high-quality children's books, call 1-800-341-3569 (USA) or 1-800-461-9120 (Canada).

Library of Congress Cataloging-in-Publication Data

Clement, Rod.
      Counting on Frank / written and illustrated by Rod Clement.
         p.   cm.
      Summary: A boy and his dog present amusing counting, size comparison, and mathematical facts.
      ISBN 0-8368-0358-2
      1. Counting—Juvenile literature. 2. Size perception—Juvenile literature. [1. Mathematics.
2. Size.] I. Title.
QA113.C53 1991
513.5'5—dc20   90-27558

North American edition first published in 1991 by
Gareth Stevens Publishing
1555 North RiverCenter Drive, Suite 201
Milwaukee, Wisconsin 53212, USA

U.S. edition copyright © 1991. First published in Australia in 1990 by William Collins Pty. Ltd., Sydney, in association with Anne Ingram Books. Text and illustrations copyright © 1990 by Rod Clement. End matter copyright © 1992 by Gareth Stevens, Inc.

Editorial consultant: Bonnie Edwards, early childhood and math resource teacher, Milwaukee Public Schools

Printed in the United States of America

4 5 6 7 8 9 95 94 93

COUNTING *on* FRANK

Written and illustrated by
ROD CLEMENT

Gareth Stevens Publishing
MILWAUKEE

My dad says, "You have a brain. Use it!" So I do.

I sit down and fill my notebook with facts.
Did you know that the average ball-point pen
draws a line seven thousand feet long
before the ink runs out?
My parents consider this fact to be
a bit childish, but I'm sure the
pen company would like to know.

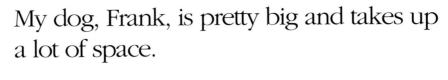

My dog, Frank, is pretty big and takes up
a lot of space.

I calculate that twenty-four Franks could fit
into my bedroom.

But sometimes there isn't even room for one.

If Frank were a humpback whale, however, only ten would fit into our entire house. I asked Dad about this, and he said they would get in the way of the television.

I calculate that only one Dad would fit inside our big television, but only one-tenth of him would fit in Mom's portable television.

Mom said she would prefer the top part because Dad's feet smell.

We've got a tree in our yard. It grows about six feet every year.

If I had grown at the same speed, I'd now be almost fifty feet tall! I wouldn't really mind, except that I'd never get clothes to fit.

I don't mind taking a bath — it gives me time to think.

For example, I calculate it would take eleven hours and forty-five minutes to fill the entire bathroom with water. That's with both faucets running.

It would take slightly less time to empty, as long as no one opened the door.

When I get dressed, I don't think about fashion or style.
I think about facts.

For instance, it's a fact that if I put on every piece of
clothing in my closet, I would be nine feet tall and
six feet wide.

I would also be unable to
sit down.

I enjoy dinner, not because of the delicious chops Mom cooks every night or the conversation. . . .

It's the peas.

If I had accidentally knocked fifteen peas off my plate every night for the last eight years, they would now be level with the table top.

Maybe then, Mom would understand that her son does *not* like peas.

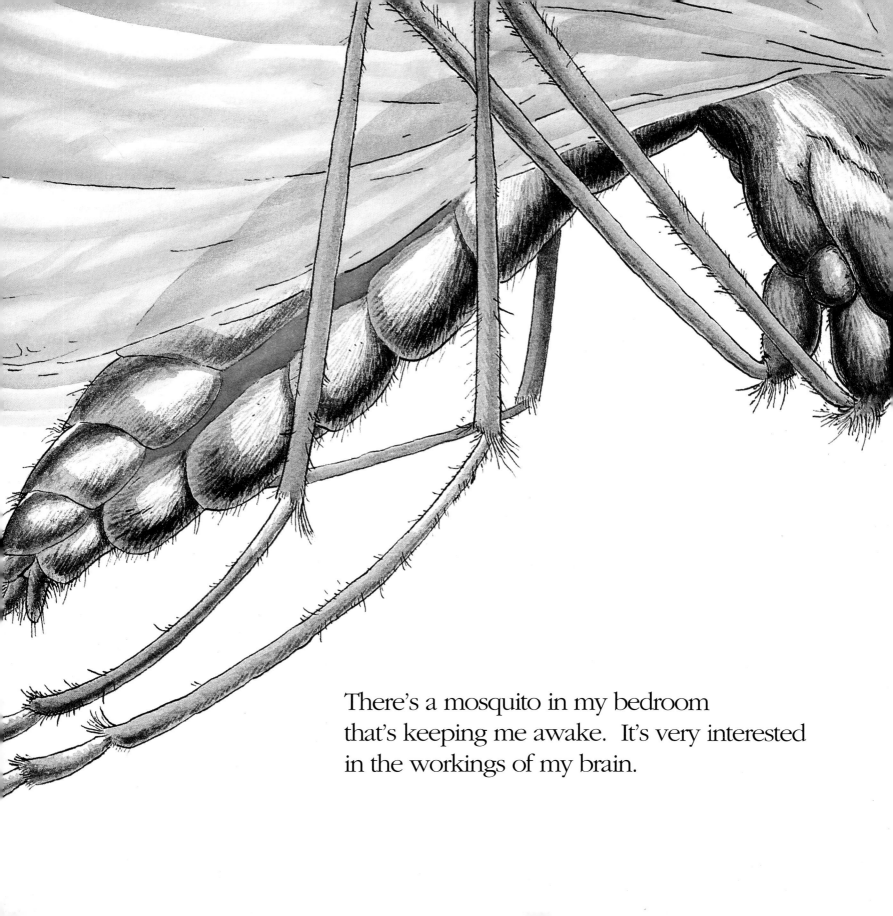

There's a mosquito in my bedroom
that's keeping me awake. It's very interested
in the workings of my brain.

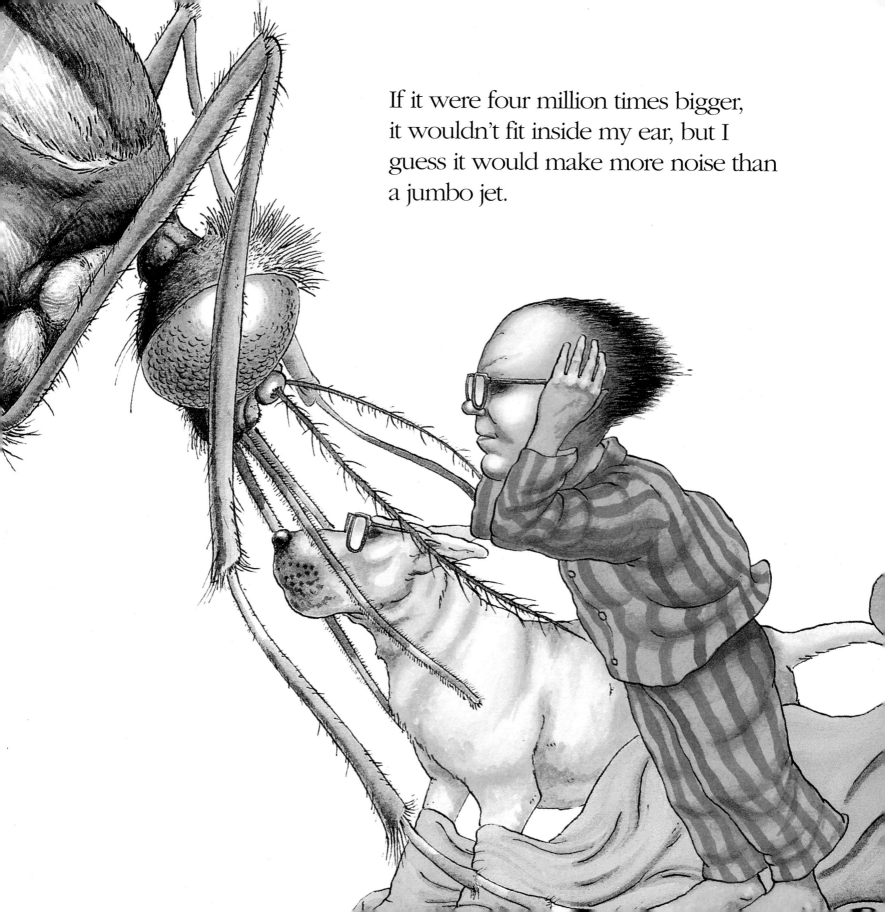

If it were four million times bigger,
it wouldn't fit inside my ear, but I
guess it would make more noise than
a jumbo jet.

At breakfast, I have a glass of orange juice and two pieces of toast.

Our old toaster shoots the toast about three feet into the air.

It makes you think — if our toaster were as big as the house, it could endanger low-flying aircraft.

Going shopping with Mom is a big event. She is lucky to have such an intelligent helper.

It takes forty-seven cans of dog food to fill one shopping bag, but only one Frank to knock over one hundred and ten!

Because of Frank, my knuckles will scrape along the ground by the time I'm twenty-five!

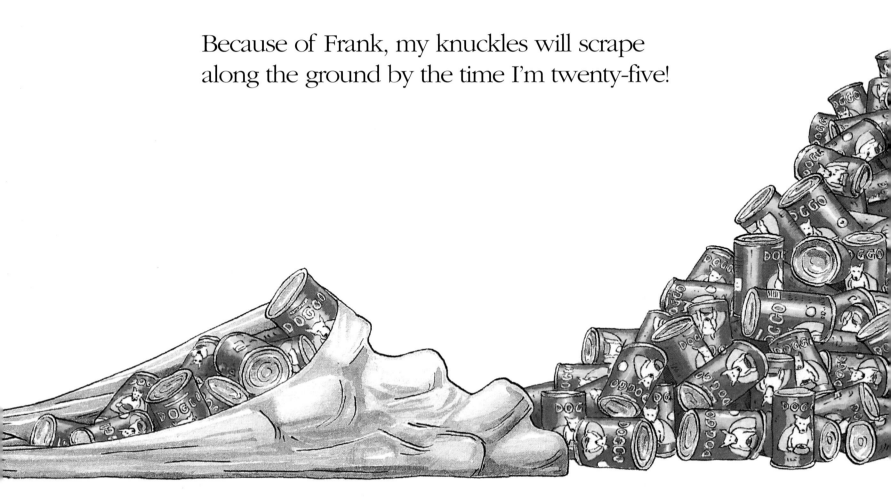

The local club had a competition. You had to guess how many jellybeans were in a jar, and the prize was a trip to Hawaii.

They didn't know who they were dealing with.

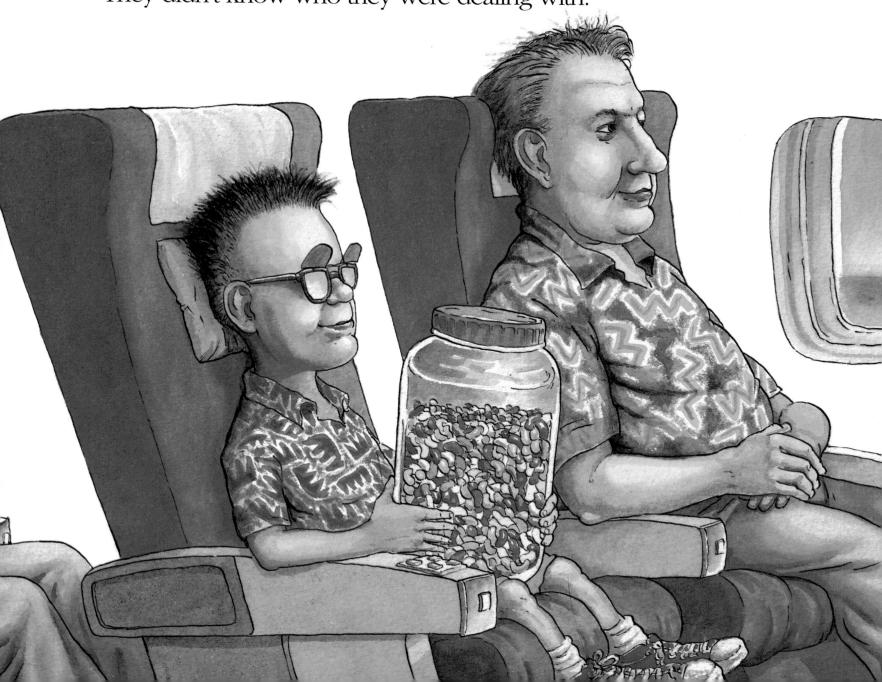

There are seven hundred and forty-five jellybeans in the average candy jar. I thought everybody knew that!

As Dad said on the plane to Hawaii,
"You have a brain. Use it!"

Here's a Chance to Use YOUR Brain!

More interesting info: English vs. metric units of measure

The units of distance in this book are given in feet. These units are part of the English system of measure. Another system of measure is the metric system. You might have learned the metric system in school. You may even be more familiar with the metric system than with the English system. Here are the rounded metric equivalents of the English measurements used in *Counting on Frank:*

This unit of English measure	gives this unit of metric measure
7000 feet	2100 meters
6 feet	1.8 meters
50 feet	15 meters
9 feet	2.5 meters
3 feet	1 meter

The fun activities that follow will give you a chance to use math and numbers in fun ways — just like Frank's friend, "the boy." **(See the bottom of the last page for the answers to the following counting problems. If you ever have trouble understanding a question or its answer, ask a grown-up for help.)**

A roomful of Franks

1. Frank's "pet" boy calculates that twenty-four Franks could fit into his bedroom. What if, in addition to these twenty-four Franks, thirty Franks could fit into the boy's parents' bedroom, twenty-five in the living room, ten in the bathroom, and twenty in the kitchen? How many Franks in all would fit into the boy's house?

2. If eight of these Franks went out for a walk, how many would that leave in the house?

3. If there were twenty-four Franks in the bedroom, how many of his ears would there be?

4. How many Frank paws would there be?

5. Find the picture of the boy in his crowded bedroom. Look closely at the piece of paper the boy is counting on. Each set of lines with a slash going through it stands for five Franks. Can you figure out how many Franks the boy has counted so far?

6. How many Franks can **you** count in this picture?

7. How many pairs of eyeglasses can you count in the picture?

"It's the peas . . ."

1. If the boy accidentally knocks fifteen peas off his plate each night, how many peas would he knock off in one week, or **seven** nights?

2. And at this rate, how many peas would he then knock off his plate in **two weeks**, or **fourteen nights**?

No more peas, please!

Now what about all the peas that **don't** fall off the plate? Let's say that each night, the boy's mom opens up one can of peas for dinner. And let's say that this can holds exactly three hundred peas. So if fifteen of these three hundred peas fall on the floor, how many peas are left in the can each night to fill the tummies of the boy, his mom and dad, and Frank?

(Dog) food for thought

1. Frank will eat only Doggo dog food, so his human family must take along enough to keep him fed and fit for their vacation in Hawaii. Frank eats two cans of Doggo a day. Including travel time, he and his family will be gone for eight days. This means that the boy must pack **sixteen** cans of Doggo for Frank. But his suitcase only holds **ten** cans. How many cans must the boy pack in another suitcase to make sixteen cans in all?

2. Doggo dog food usually sells for about $1.50 a can. If Frank eats two cans a day, how much money will Frank's family have to spend per day to feed Frank?

3. The boy plans to divide up his 745 jelly beans evenly over each day of the trip. What would happen if he decided to eat **all** of his jelly beans on the **same** day?

More counting fun

1. You may need a grown-up to help you with this one: Have a counting contest with your friends or family. Fill a measuring cup with dry macaroni noodles. Can you guess how many noodles it takes to fill the cup? Write down everyone's guess and count the noodles to see who is closest to being right.

2. You might try the same macaroni-counting exercise as in number one above, this time with a cup of **cooked** macaroni. Now you can see how much the noodles expand when they're boiled. *(Important: Be careful around hot stoves. Be sure a grown-up is present to help you cook the noodles.)*

3. Here's a pea-counting contest you can have with your family and friends. Ask a grown-up to open a can of peas. Empty the peas into a clear measuring cup or glass, and try to guess the number of peas that were in the can. (Any size can will do, but remember, when you're done, you'll have to count the peas, and you **may even** have to eat them!)

4. What if **you** grew as fast as the boy, at the rate of six feet (1.8 meters) each year since you were born? How tall would **you** be on your next birthday? (You might need a grown-up to help you figure this one out.)

5. The next time you eat fruit with seeds, such as an apple, an orange, or a piece of watermelon, count the seeds. Besides finding out how many seeds your fruit contains, you can have a contest with a friend or relative to see whose fruit has the most seeds.

Answers (Use a mirror to check your answers!)

A Roomful of Franks
1. (100 Franks!)
2. (101 Franks)
3. (48 ears)
4. (60 paws)
5. (39 Franks)
6. (Some people have found as many as 20 Franks, but the number changes each time we count!)
7. (16 pairs — 15 are on Frank, and one is on the boy)

"...It's the peas..."
1. (105 peas)   2. (210 peas)
No more peas, please!
(285 peas left in the can)
Dog food for thought (Dog)
1. (6 cans)
2. ($3.00)
3. (He'd have a terrible stomach ache, of course!)

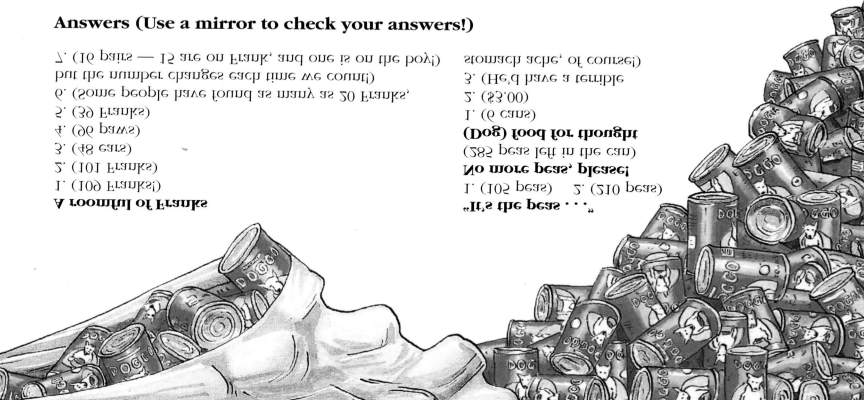